S0-DRD-977

Snowshoe Thompson
Sierra Mailman

Snowshoe Thompson
Sierra Mailman

John L. Smith

KEYSTONE
CANYON PRESS

KEYSTONE
CANYON PRESS

Publisher Alrica Goldstein
Editor Paul Szydelko
Cover Designer Alissa Booth
Cartographer David Stroud
Picture Research Catherine Magee

Keystone Canyon Press
2341 Crestone Drive
Reno, NV 89523

www.keystonecanyon.com

Copyright © 2020 by John L. Smith

All rights reserved. No part of this book may be reproduced in any manner whatsoever without written permission except in the case of brief quotations embodied in critical articles and reviews.

The publisher would like to thank the Nevada Historical Society, the Nevada State Museum, Nevada State Parks, University of Nevada Archives, and the Library of Congress for their kind permission to take and reproduce photographs. Chapter openers: Vecteezy.com; p. 18: ID 77896453 © Larry Gevert | Dreamstime.com; p.25: 109918636 © creativecommonsstockphotos | Dreamstime.com

A Cataloging-in-Publication record for this title is available from the Library of Congress.

ISBN 978-1-953055-00-2
EPUB ISBN 978-1-953055-02-6

Manufactured in the United States of America

For my father P. L. Smith
and my stepsons Ralph, Grant, and Carson
—always at home in the Sierra Nevada

Table of Contents

Timeline

1827   On April 30, Jon Torsteinson-Rue is born in Tinn, Prestijeld, Norway.

1837   He comes to the United States with his family and settles for a short time in Illinois. His parents change their name to Thompson. Young Jon becomes John A. Thompson (sometimes spelled Thomson.)

1841   The Thompson family moves to Iowa.

1845   The Thompson family returns to Illinois before moving on to Missouri.

1851   Thompson, now 24, decides to strike out from Missouri to the gold fields of California.

1855   Thompson learns of the danger and difficulty experienced by those who attempted to deliver mail over the snowy Sierra Nevada mountains during the treacherous winter months.

1856   On January 3, Snowshoe answers an advertisement in a Sacramento, California newspaper and accepts the job of delivering the mail in the middle of winter across the frozen Sierra Nevada and sets off on his first trip.

1857   Thompson encounters a pack of timber wolves on his way to the Carson Valley.

1858   On December 18, the first issue of the *Territorial Enterprise* goes to press in Genoa after Thompson helps deliver the lead type and parts of the printing press. The newspaper is later published in Virginia City.

1860 Thompson fights alongside Major William Ormsby in the Pyramid Lake War with the Northern Paiute. Ormsby is killed. Thompson escapes injury.

1864 On October 31, Nevada officially becomes the thirty-sixth state.

1865 Civil War ends.

1866 Thompson becomes a US citizen, homesteads a 160-acre ranch in Diamond Valley, California. He marries Agnes Singleton of England.

1867 On February 11, the Thompsons' only son, Arthur Thomas, is born in Genoa.

1868 Thompson travels to Washington, DC, in an attempt to persuade government officials to give him just compensation for his efforts at delivering the mail. He is denied payment, but continues to deliver the mail anyway.

1868-1872 Thompson is a member of the Alpine County (California) Board of Supervisors.

1876 Snowshoe makes his last mail delivery. After a short illness, possibly related to appendicitis and pneumonia, but described by one account as a "liver ailment," Thompson dies on May 15 at his ranch in Diamond Valley, California. He is buried in the cemetery at Genoa, Nevada.

1886 The October 8 edition of popular *Overland Monthly* magazine features a lengthy article on the exploits of Snowshoe Thompson, written by the celebrated journalist and short-story writer Dan DeQuille.

x

Map of Northern Nevada/California

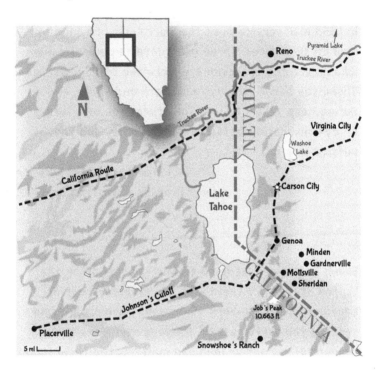

In 1853 mail service over the Sierra was provided by men on snowshoes. Three years later a powerful man who gained the affectionate nickname of "Snowshoe" Thompson began to carry mail back and forth, and during deep snows he was sometimes the only means of communication between Carson Valley and the outside world.

— writers associated with the
Work Projects Administration, 1940.

Skiing had as yet made no serious impression on the United States . . . There was, however, one skier in California: Norway-born "Snowshoe Thompson," who recalled the usefulness of the long narrow wooden runners of his native land and constructed them from memory. When blizzards walled the gold camps in with snow, Snowshoe Thompson was able to penetrate with a rescue kit of food and supplies. . . . Californians regarded Thompson with as much awe as if he had suddenly sprouted wings and begun to fly.

— writer, historian Elizabeth Margo, 1955.

Chapter One

A Letter From Home

The discovery of gold in January 1848 at Sutter's Mill in Coloma, California, less than 100 miles from modern-day Carson City, Nevada, set off a rush of migration of 300,000 people to the area from across the United States. Fortune-seekers in the West found themselves far from home in an unsettled land where communicating with family and friends meant sending a letter on a very long journey.

Timely communication was one of the great challenges on the American frontier. In the days well before the internet and telephone, and even before the telegraph was widely used, sending a letter to a loved one or business partner was expensive and time-consuming.

Conversations that we take for granted were impossible. Making connections over long distances was extremely difficult and took weeks, even months. Mail was often lost along the way. And even when it reached its general destination, it often piled up undelivered because the person who was addressed

1

couldn't be found.

Before the nation had highways or even dirt roads, the most direct mail routes from east to west were more than 2,500 miles long with the final 1,600 miles crossing the great American frontier. Several routes on the latter part of the journey were used, but after the Civil War began in 1861 the "Central Route" from St. Joseph, Missouri, to Placerville, California, in the Sierra Nevada foothills' "Gold Country" became popular. Pulled by four-horse and eight-horse teams, Overland Mail Company stagecoaches hauled letters, packages, and people on the brutally bumpy journey. Inside the crowded coaches, up to 20 passengers sat in narrow rows of wooden benches uncomfortably close together for hour after hour. The average speed of the stagecoach? Just five miles per hour.

With breaks only to change horses and drivers, the stages often traveled twenty-four hours a day and reached their destination in twenty-five days. As difficult as it was to travel at any time, the trip was worse in winter when the trail was often impassable. And when heavy snows fell, travel ceased entirely.

Other routes existed, but they were much longer.

One route went by sea all the way from the Atlantic Ocean around Cape Horn at the tip of South America and into the Pacific Ocean, eventually making its way to San Francisco, and a final leg to Placerville. In all, it was a journey of approximately 13,500 miles. A third route was shorter, but even more dangerous: south to

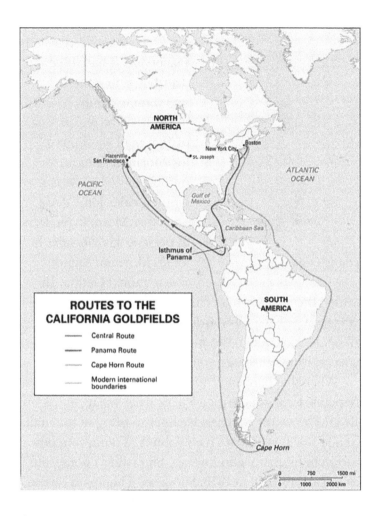

ROUTES TO THE CALIFORNIA GOLDFIELDS

—— Central Route

••••• Panama Route

----- Cape Horn Route

—— Modern international boundaries

Panama by ship, across the jungles of the Isthmus of Panama by horseback or on foot (long before the Canal was built in 1914), then back on a ship and north to San Francisco. Both trips took months to complete in the best of weather.

John "Snowshoe" Thompson

Once the mail reached Placerville, it had to be distributed to settlements and mining camps throughout the region. Some of that mail was bound for Mormon Station, an outpost settled by Mormon Church elder John Reese and other Morman pioneers in present-day Nevada. In 1855, Mormon Station was renamed Genoa. In winter, the final stretch of the journey from Placerville to Genoa was the most arduous of all. The Sierra was all but blocked when the snow fell, and Genoa became isolated from outside contact.

When that happened, the townsfolk found themselves desperate for a stouthearted letter carrier willing to risk his life and brave the harshest weather to bring in the mail. Genoa was fortunate to have John A. Thompson, best known to his many admirers as "Snowshoe Thompson." From January 1856 to 1876, Snowshoe Thompson carried letters and packages in his backpack over the Sierra Nevada mountain range from California to Nevada for little and often no pay. He traveled alone even in the worst weather. He never got lost, and he never lost a single letter.

Snowshoe Thompson was truly at home in the high Sierra.

4

Chapter 2

Here Comes Snowshoe!

The people of Genoa and the Carson Valley were a sturdy bunch. They were accustomed to hardship in winter, when the snows were sometimes heavy and the temperatures often fell below freezing for many days at a time.

When the first snows came, communication with towns and cities in California to the west and the Utah Territory to the east often ceased. They were isolated. There was no reliable way to ride a horse over the snow-packed Sierra Nevada, and to attempt to walk over the mountains was considered a foolish and deadly exercise.

Prospectors and fur trappers often froze to death in those high mountains. Even the Northern Paiute people, who had lived in the region for centuries, stayed out of the Sierra in winter.

Settlers and Native Americans alike knew well the story of the ill-fated Donner Party, which tried to cross the Sierra in winter but was stranded by heavy snowfall. The Donner Party (1846–1847) lost many members of its group to the bitter cold weather and deep snow. They became so starved for food that some of the most desperate ate their leather shoes and even the flesh of their dead.

By 1856, it had been only thirty years since mountain men such as Jim Bridger and Peter Skene Ogden had first crossed the Sierra. Only a dozen years earlier Captain John C. Frémont and his expedition mapped the region with help on the trail from Kit Carson and the Northern Paiute chief, Captain Truckee.

Yes, the Sierra Nevada in winter was a dangerous place.

So imagine their surprise when the residents of Genoa and the Carson Valley first learned of the approach of the man who had somehow managed to cross those mountains and bring them their mail. Residents would come to call him "Snowshoe Thompson."

They sometimes heard him before they saw him. Snowshoe Thompson would let out a "whoop" that echoed through the high passes and halfway down into the valley.

If conditions were right, Thompson would strap his feet onto long, narrow planks of wood he called snowshoes, but today we would call cross-country skis. Using a six-foot-long pole to help his balance, he'd push off from a high ridge and come rushing downhill from Genoa Peak like a man possessed. In a time before there were such things as ski lodges and snowboarders, he was a rare and incredible sight.

Thompson coming down the mountain.

The townsfolk immediately dropped what they were doing. They left dinner plates on the table and chores undone and hurried to witness his mastery of the steep mountainside. As he came closer, people could see that he was a tall, handsome fellow with blond hair and beard. He was six feet tall and weighed 180 pounds, far above average for his era. He wore a floppy hat with a wide brim and a lightweight Mackinaw coat. He covered his face with charcoal to protect against the snow's potentially blinding glare. He carried no rifle or pistol. As he came closer still, they could see that he had bright blue eyes and a big smile on his face.

On his back were strapped large leather bags containing mail and other items. In total, the bags normally weighed sixty to eighty pounds, but on one occasion topped 100 pounds. The bags contained dozens of letters and packages. They often included cooking pots, the lead type for the printing press of

7

Mail bags like these would have carried letters back and forth between California and Utah territory.

Virginia City's *Territorial Enterprise* newspaper, and silver ore samples from mines that would become famous as "the Comstock Lode." There were letters from distant relatives, stories of births, marriages, and deaths in families. There were letters detailing the latest developments at the gold mines and mills of California, which had attracted thousands of people from across the United States. He even carried a kerosene lamp to the door of an elderly woman with poor eyesight so that she might be able to better see her evening sewing.

Those who looked at Thompson closely would notice that he carried no tent. He stayed warm on his difficult journey by building a fire with matches safely stored in a tin box. On his trip, he ate biscuits, beef jerky, and dried sausage that needed no cooking. For water, he melted snow or drank from the streams and springs he found along the way. He didn't even bother to carry a water jug.

Snowshoe Thompson certainly wasn't afraid of the dark. He often walked day and night to reach his destination. And even heavy snowstorms didn't deter him, but instead gave him an opportunity to test his amazing snowshoe skis.

Observers would marvel at Thompson's skill. He was once timed traveling 1,600 feet in just twenty-one seconds on a downhill run—an amazing fifty-two miles per hour. And his longest jump was measured at a remarkable 180 feet.

He was capable of walking many miles without rest, but not even a person as strong as Thompson could make the ninety-mile journey one way without a break. When it was time to bed down for the night, he found an old tree stump and collected dry branches for a campfire. Once it was built, he gathered pine branches and set them lengthwise like a bed near the fire. Placing his head on the sacks of mail, he buttoned his Mackinaw coat, pulled his broad-brimmed hat over his eyes, warmed his feet by the fire, and enjoyed a well-deserved nap. At times he slept comfortably atop many feet of snow.

Snowshoe also had a few secret places he used when he needed to rest for the evening. He would sometimes stay in one of the abandoned cabins left by miners and mountaineers who couldn't handle the rugged Sierra winters. He also took shelter in small caves, where his pine-branch bed and small campfire were drier and even more comforting to him.

But he wasn't there to hibernate like the grizzly and black bears that lived in the great mountains. Soon he was back on the snowy trail, pushing toward his destination.

Once he reached the end of the line and distributed the mail, he rested for a short time in a real bed. Then he loaded up his pack and set off on the ninety-mile return trip.

How did he learn to become so comfortable in such harsh conditions?

For that answer, we must go back to Snowshoe's childhood.

Chapter 3

From Norway to Nevada

It is fitting that a man of John Thompson's fame and familiarity with snow would be born in Norway, one of the colder countries on Earth. He was born Jon Torsteinson-Rue in the village of Tinn on April 30, 1827. At that time of year, the ground is still frozen and blanketed with late spring snow. Tinn is located in the Telemark region of Norway, an area that even then was renowned for its residents' ability to ski and skate over the snow and ice. It was there that the young boy strapped on his first pair of what Norwegians called "ski skates."

The Torsteinson-Rue family remained in Norway until 1837, when it immigrated to the United States and settled in Illinois. The family moved to Iowa a short time later, then returned to Illinois before pressing on to Missouri. By then they called themselves Thompson.

Young John Thompson was a strong, healthy man with a heart for adventure. By the late 1840s, he moved

11

from Missouri to Wisconsin to help his brother run a dairy farm. From far off to the west, word had spread throughout America of the discovery of gold at Sutter's Mill in California. Gold fever was rampant, and young Thompson decided to seek his fortune. He did so in an uncommon way—by herding milk cows from Wisconsin to California. He honed his survival skills by hunting deer and trapping birds along the way.

Thompson worked the gold fields outside Placerville, California and was employed on mining claims called Georgetown, Coon Hollow, and Kelsey Diggings. He saved what little money he made and bought a small ranch in the Sacramento Valley. He had certainly come a long way from his home in Norway.

Here Thompson's story might have ended if he had not read an advertisement in *The Sacramento Union* newspaper:

People Lost to the World; Uncle Sam Needs a Mail Carrier

The advertisement called for a special person capable of braving harsh winter weather to deliver the mail to isolated communities in the Sierra Nevada mountains and as far away as the Carson Valley. It was not work for the weak of heart. Thompson must have realized he was the perfect person for the job. He also was sensitive to the need for timely mail service, for it had taken many months for the letter that informed him of his mother's death to reach him.

After turning Thompson down several times, the postmaster finally gave the young man a chance, but according to one account told him, "I'm sorry, the contract carrier is the only one who can sign the contract over to you. And he just vanished. I don't have the authority to hire you." It amounted to a handshake deal, and it was an arrangement that Thompson would later regret.

Thompson wasn't the first person to attempt to deliver the mail over the Sierra in winter. Several years earlier, mountain man John Calhoun Johnson, known throughout the region as "Sierra John," had found the most reliable path through the icy passes from Placerville to the Carson Valley. Although often clogged with snowdrifts up to fifty feet deep, "Johnson's Cutoff" was the closest thing to a highway through those dangerous mountains. It wasn't a road, however, just a path through the mountains.

Others had tried to emulate Johnson, and a few had succeeded, but some paid a heavy price for their efforts. Most had quit after a single trip. One was killed in a fight with Indians. Whether using circular-shaped Canadian-style snowshoes, sometimes called "webs" because of their resemblance to spider webs, or attempting to cut a path through the deep snow for their pack animals, their best efforts resulted in frustration, lengthy delays in mail delivery, and frozen fingers and toes.

Even explorers as skilled and experienced as John C. Frémont and Kit Carson crossed the Sierra in winter with great difficulty. Frémont's 1844 expedition entered the Sierra in late winter and encountered deep snow. Fortunately, Frémont's trusted friend Carson was an experienced mountain man who had learned to craft snowshoes out of pine boughs from Native Americans in the Rocky Mountains. Once they were attached to their feet, the snowshoes kept the men from sinking.

Frémont's sixty-five-member group could do little to keep their horses and mules from sinking into the snow. Frémont ordered his men to use their shovels to pack down the snow to give the animals more solid footing, but that meant cutting a trail all the way through the mountains. It could take days to travel a single mile.

Frémont's trail-hardened group took more than fifteen days to cross the Sierra Nevada from the Carson Valley to the Sacramento Valley and lost all but a few of their pack animals.

Thompson had a plan to succeed where others had struggled. He had learned to use his "ski-skates" as a boy in Norway. Although there had been no chance to practice in the flatlands of Illinois, Iowa, Missouri, and Wisconsin, the Sierra Nevada was an ideal location.

With winter approaching, he set out to find the appropriate material to make a pair. They would be made of oak. He cut long planks to the proper length—almost ten feet long, three inches wide, and one-inch thick—and carved them into the proper shape. They weighed twenty-five pounds, but when conditions were right they glided over the surface of

Most covered wagons rode on wheels like these made of wood with iron rims that sometimes separated from the wood. A typical wagon weighed more than 3,000 pounds fully loaded and needed the iron to support them.

the snow. He added a long pole to balance himself.

As 1855 came to an end, Thompson practiced on his skis in the hills outside Placerville. In the new year, it was time for him to test his "snowshoes" and his own endurance.

Townspeople and newspaper reporters were skeptical. They had seen other strong men fail in their best efforts to hike through the snow. They wondered whether this time would be different. Thompson accepted the risky job believing that the federal government would fairly compensate him for his efforts. He set off on his first mail run on January 3, 1856.

He left Placerville that morning to cheers and skepticism. A resident is believed to have called out, "Good luck, Snowshoe Thompson."

The name stuck.

Would his amazing snow skis serve him well, or send him off the trail and into the pine trees? No one but Thompson himself knew for certain.

The journey took him from Placerville into the mountains, across Johnson's Cutoff, and down into Mormon Station, more commonly known as Genoa. The ninety-mile distance in one direction had defeated previous carriers. One had quit after suffering from frostbite and fatigue from his journey, which had taken him eight days to complete. With the aid of his skis and a greater understanding of the mountains, Snowshoe Thompson covered the same ground in just three days—thirty miles a day through the snow. He made his return trip with a lighter pack in just two days.

Newspaper reporters and residents from Sacramento and Placerville were astounded at his speed, and by the fact that the trip hadn't seemed to exhaust the young man. He made thirty-one trips through the Sierra Nevada that first winter, and even added side trips to deliver letters to isolated mining camps.

The legend of Snowshoe Thompson was born.

Even in blizzard conditions Thompson made his trip up to four times per month for the next twenty winters.

Along the way, he piled up adventures even higher than the Sierra snow.

Chapter 4

At Home in the Mountains

By his second winter on the job, Snowshoe Thompson was making regular trips no matter the temperature. He often used his skis, but when the weather permitted he sometimes took a horse-drawn sleigh far into the mountains. To make it easier for the horses, he sometimes packed down the snow in their path. He used his skis during shorter side trips to deliver the mail to isolated mining camps and ranches. He understood the importance of adapting to rapidly changing conditions in the weather and on the ground.

Although Thompson was best known as the "Sierra Postman," he sometimes acted as a newspaper carrier for Nevada's famous *Territorial Enterprise*. In fact, he delivered the lead type used in the *Enterprise's* printing press and often packed copies of the newspaper over the mountains to Placerville. He not only made news, but delivered it too.

Through the years Snowshoe carried sewing needles, glassware, cooking pots, books, fiddle strings,

Noted author Mark Twain wrote for the *Territorial Enterprise* newspaper in the 1860s in Virginia City, Nevada.

and even a "peep stone," a stone with a hole in the middle with which some people claimed they could predict future events. He jammed many things into his leather pouches.

He also played a role in the greatest mining discovery in Nevada history. When gold prospectors Peter O'Reilly and Pat McLaughlin unearthed a heavy blue ore from their mining claim outside the Carson Valley, they had no idea what it was. So they entrusted a sample of the blue rock to Thompson, who carried it over the mountains and into Placerville to be studied. The blue rock turned out to be silver ore, and the discovery led to the development of the

Comstock Lode and a mining boom that eventually led to Nevada's statehood and its nickname, the Silver State.

As the Johnson's Cutoff route became more established, the camps of a few miners and settlers dotted the mountainsides. But when the heavy snows came, even the most stubborn people were advised to come down into the warmer valleys. After all, snow at the crest was known to pile fifty feet deep, and winter blizzards blew up to eighty miles per hour.

Sierra Nevada is Spanish for "Snowy Mountains." It stretches more than 400 miles from south to north on California's eastern edge and is roughly 70 miles wide. To the west of the Sierra is California's Central Valley. To the east lies the Great Basin and Nevada.

The peaks of the Sierra Nevada vary greatly in elevation from about 5,000 feet up to 14,505 at Mount Whitney, the highest point in the United States outside Alaska. The elevation of the area that Snowshoe Thompson traveled through at Johnson's Cutoff was approximately 8,000 feet.

Although he sometimes saw fresh bear tracks in the snow, Thompson ran little risk of encountering the grizzly and black bears that roamed the Sierra because the animals hibernated in winter. In all the winters he traveled alone through the mountains Thompson was never afraid—except on one occasion when he came across a pack of six hungry timber wolves.

They were big animals with long legs and thick winter coats. We know today that wolves don't attack people, and in fact do their best to avoid them. As a boy growing up in Norway, however, Thompson had been raised listening to folk tales about ferocious wolves that tricked children and sometimes ate them. He had even heard wild stories of werewolves, men who turn into wolves during the full moon. It was pretty scary stuff. Today, of course, we know werewolves are only make-believe.

Small children still read the story of "Little Red Riding Hood," in which a little girl barely escapes from a wolf with big teeth. Thompson saw the big teeth of the six wolves and was afraid.

The wolves were pawing through the snow to uncover the carcass of a dead deer when Thompson encountered them. They looked at him, and his childhood fears began to rise. He knew he must not run away or show weakness, for he believed the wolves would sense his fear and might attack him.

"To my eyes, those before me looked to have hair on them a foot long," Thompson recalled many years later to the famous *Territorial Enterprise* reporter Dan DeQuille.

The wolves turned away from the carcass and watched Thompson closely. Following their pack leader, they trotted closer to him and promptly sat about thirty yards away. He believed they were sizing him up,

Wolves primarily work together in packs to bring down large prey animals such as deer and elk in the Sierra Nevada. Wolves are beginning to return to these mountains after being hunted out over 100 years ago.

perhaps for a delicious winter meal.

"Just when I was opposite them . . . the leader of the pack threw back his head, and uttered a loud and prolonged howl," he remembered. "All the others of the pack did the same. 'Ya-hoo! Ya-oo, woo-oo!' cried all together. A more doleful and terrific sound I never heard. I thought it meant my death. The awful cry rang across the silent valley, was echoed by the hills, and re-echoed far away among the surrounding mountains."

Although he was afraid inside, outwardly Thompson showed no fear. Instead, he marched away from the animals.

"They sat still and watched me hungrily for some time, but when I was far away I saw them all turn about and go back to the carcass," he said. "My show of courage intimidated them and kept them back."

The wolves were frightening, but travelers through the Sierra in winter knew they had far more to fear from the heavy snows and cold temperatures. Sometimes when conditions were too difficult and Thompson was not near a favorite cave or abandoned cabin, he would find a stable place under a tree and perform a hopping Norwegian folk dance. For hours he would jump up and down to keep warm. He must have been quite a sight all alone in the high mountains dancing and sometimes singing as the snow fell and the winds howled like hungry wolves.

During all his trips in the harshest of weather conditions, he kept his sense of direction. Thompson was not only very familiar with his mountains, but he also had developed what might be called a strong inner compass. He had learned to read his environment for signs like moss growing on the north side of trees and rocks or using the position of the sun and stars in the sky.

"I can't be lost!" Thompson exclaimed to DeQuille. "I can go anywhere in the mountains, day or night, storm or shine. I've got something in here that keeps me right. I have found many persons who were lost—dozens of men, first and last—but I have never been lost myself. There is no danger of being lost in a narrow range of mountains like the Sierra, if a man has his wits about him."

Over the years, many men who failed to keep their wits about them needed to be rescued by Snowshoe Thompson.

Chapter 5

A Friend on the Trail

The Sierra's snow-covered pine forests were as familiar to Snowshoe Thompson as a person's own backyard, but few people who ventured into the Sierra Nevada could say the same. During his twenty years of mail delivery, Thompson found many lost travelers and saved the lives of at least seven men who surely would have perished without his help. Some people reported they became confused after fresh snow covered familiar trails and landmarks.

Others lost their sense of direction in the deep canyons. When one miner in Lake Valley attempted to return to civilization, he left his simply constructed cabin each morning and walked all day only to find himself back in the same place by nightfall. He had walked in a full circle. Day after day he went out and returned to the same spot. After four days, he grew weaker and was losing hope.

"I have found a great many lost men, and have rescued some men when they were at death's door,"

Snowshoe recalled. "He knew nothing about the course of the prevailing winds, about trees and rocks, or about the stars in the heavens, not to speak of the formation and configuration of the mountains."

Fortunately for the miner from Lake Valley, Snowshoe read the mountains like a book.

One of Thompson's most famous rescues came when he saved the life of a stranded packer named James Sissons, who had become injured and ill during a snowstorm and was trapped in his isolated cabin.

During Thompson's mail run through a heavy snowstorm just two days before Christmas in 1856, he entered a cabin he thought was abandoned and found Sissons freezing to death inside. His boots were frozen to his feet. His fire was cold. He had burned all his wood and was unable to get more. He had almost run out of food, such as it was. He had survived twelve days on raw flour. The injured man was waiting to die, but praying to live.

Thompson would recall weeks later that Sissons' pain must have been indescribable, but he didn't cry out or even complain. As one writer explained it in 1857, "Although death would soon have terminated his agony, he still had a lingering hope that Providence might direct Mr. Thompson by his cabin, and thus save him." Had Thompson not decided to stop at the cabin that night, Sissons almost certainly would have died.

Instead, Thompson sized up the problem and quickly saw that Sissons was too large and too injured to carry on his back. Snowshoe, as strong as he was,

James Sissons was rescued from a cabin piled high with snow like this.

would need help with the life-or-death task.

He collected enough firewood to keep the cabin warm. Then he supplied Sissons with enough water and what little food was available. Then he returned to the trail.

Thompson fought his way through the snowstorm, over the mountain, and down into Genoa, where he swiftly assembled a group of volunteers to serve as a rescue team. They made a simple bed on which to carry the injured man and returned to the cabin without resting. By the time Thompson returned, Sissons' condition had worsened.

The rescuers loaded up the man and carried him back down to Genoa, where a doctor examined him and determined that his two gangrenous legs would have to be amputated, or cut off, so he could live. Gangrene is when tissues within the body die because of a lack of blood supply. But the doctor had no chloroform, the chemical physicians used back then to make patients unconscious before surgery. Without the chloroform, the operation would have killed Sissons. The nearest supply was back over the mountains more than 100 miles away in Sacramento, California.

Thompson knew what he had to do. He set out immediately and returned to the snowy hills, crossing them in record time and dropping down into Placerville ninety miles away. Then it was on to Sacramento, where he obtained the chloroform and returned to Genoa the only way possible—on foot and using his snowshoes.

When he reached Genoa, the doctor immediately set to work. Although James Sissons' feet suffered severe gangrene and had to be amputated, he survived the operation and lived many more years thanks to the incredible postman of the Sierra Nevada.

Perhaps the most celebrated person rescued by Thompson was Elias "Lucky" Baldwin, who would become a multimillionaire landowner and developer in San Francisco and Los Angeles. Baldwin was known for building hotels, theaters, and the Santa Anita thoroughbred horseracing park. But in the winter of 1859 Baldwin set out with two companions for the mines of Nevada to dig for gold. "I had plenty of money," he recalled, "but I wanted some mining excitement."

He experienced far more excitement than he bargained for.

As he climbed through the Sierra, the snow began to fall. As the storm worsened, Baldwin's trail disappeared. It fell so fast they couldn't see their tracks behind them. They were stranded eight miles from the tiny town of Strawberry, California with one blanket each and struggled to light a small fire. They huddled under a fallen tree and searched their pockets for matches. They found just three.

"We picked twigs and limbs from the fallen tree, shook off the snow, and sheltering the blaze from the wind with our blankets we finally got a weak little flame," Baldwin remembered decades later.

Their best efforts to keep warm were failing.

"Then we snuggled into the crevice, wrapped the blankets around us, thinking that in spite of all we would freeze to death."

Sensing trouble in the mountains, the residents of Strawberry contacted their friend, Thompson, who agreed to search for the lost travelers before it was too late. He grabbed his great skis and set off.

"We were half frozen when Snowshoe found us," Baldwin recalled. "We drew straws with chattering teeth to see who should go first." Baldwin's friend Howard made the first trip. "He put his feet on the back of Thompson's snowshoes, his arms around Thompson's neck, and away they slid down the eight mountain miles to Strawberry."

At least one would get out alive, Baldwin thought, as the night grew colder. Thompson couldn't be expected to return until morning. Even though half of his trip was downhill, it was still a sixteen-mile journey.

"It was all right going down, but it was slow work for Snowshoe Thompson climbing up hill again," Baldwin said. "We thought he would never get back, and our hopes were down to zero again when we heard his cheery 'Hello!'"

By the end of a very long night and early morning, Thompson had made the round trip three times. Baldwin would go on to make and lose a fortune in real estate and development, traveling the world and piling up his own adventures. But the memory of that night in the mountains being rescued by Snowshoe Thompson remained with him the rest of his life.

"I've covered ground in a good many ways—from an elephant's back in India and a jinrikisha in Japan to the fastest coach and eight (horses) in California—but that ride on the back of those snowshoes was the most exciting one I ever had in my life. Old 'Snowshoe' Thompson didn't stop to say 'look out for corners,' and hanging on for dear life, we went sliding down the mountain. Snowshoe made the three trips one after another without a complaint, although that was a terrible hardship even for a man as accustomed to the snow-covered mountains as was Snowshoe."

Chapter 6

Heeding the Call of Duty

After making his winter mail deliveries, Snowshoe Thompson settled into his 160-acre ranch in Diamond Valley, California, about twenty miles from Genoa. Thompson cut wood to sell, raised crops, and grazed cattle, both his own and for other ranchers. He was known as a good neighbor who would help others in the field or on the range. Thompson also was a member of the local militia, a group of armed citizen soldiers whose stated duty was to defend the community.

The migration of hundreds of thousands of miners and settlers to the region following the discovery of gold and silver had a devastating impact on the Native American tribes who had called the area home for generations. The clash of cultures sometimes erupted in violence. Tensions increased throughout the late 1850s. Battles were waged between the whites against members of the Northern Paiute and other tribes.

By May 1860, with the Indians pushed farther from their traditional homes and hunting grounds, the

Pyramid Lake in Northern Nevada.

scattered violence worsened into what became known
as the Pyramid Lake War between the whites and the
Northern Paiute.

As a member of the militia, Thompson fought
under the command of Major William Ormsby,
who had a history of good relations with the Paiute,
especially tribal chief Captain Truckee and his
son-in-law, Winnemucca. To improve relations and
communication between the whites and Indians,
the Ormsby family took in Winnemucca's daughter
Sarah and taught her English. She would later use her
impressive language and communication skills to be an
advocate for her people.

Renegade Indians were suspected of killing two
men at Williams Station, a store and Pony Express
transfer point a few miles from Genoa. In response,
Ormsby gathered more than 100 militia volunteers

to retrieve and bury the bodies, and then to search for those responsible. It wasn't until later that it was learned the men had been killed after kidnapping two young Paiute girls.

Ormsby and his men followed the Truckee River in the direction of Pyramid Lake. On May 12, while traveling along the Truckee River, Ormsby and his men, including Snowshoe Thompson, were attacked by a Northern Paiute battle party of approximately 100 led by war chief Numaga. In their superior positions, the Indians had little trouble defeating Ormsby and the poorly trained volunteers, killing seventy-six in all. Ormsby was killed.

Only Thompson's strength and speed enabled him escape unharmed. He would fight in no more battles.

PONY EXPRESS

ST. JOSEPH, MISSOURI TO CALIFORNIA
IN TEN DAYS OR LESS.

WANTED

YOUNG, SKINNY, WIRY FELLOWS
NOT OVER EIGHTEEN, MUST BE
EXPERT RIDERS, WILLING TO
RISK DEATH DAILY.
ORPHANS PREFERRED.
WAGES $25 PER WEEK

**APPLY PONY EXPRESS STABLES
ST. JOSEPH, MISSOURI**

Chapter Seven

Just Compensation

With much fanfare, in April 1860 the Pony Express mail service started its horseback relay from Missouri to Sacramento, California. Back in the Sierra Nevada, Snowshoe Thompson didn't break his stride. He remained the most reliable source of mail delivery during the long Sierra winter.

But change was coming. The Central Pacific Railroad was under construction, and soon anyone with a ticket would be able to cross the Sierra in almost any weather.

While the railroad was being built, Snowshoe delivered mail from Cisco to the track workers at Meadow Lake City. Today that winding and mountainous fifty-five mile route can be traveled by automobile in about two hours. In the 1860s, Snowshoe Thompson blazed his own trail out of necessity.

At the time, Clarence M. Wooster was a young railroad telegrapher who spent long winters amid the other workers and hundreds of mules used to haul

The Pony Express Commemorative Stamp was issued in 1960.

logs and other heavy objects. In a letter to his family, Wooster recalled seeing Thompson's approach on his incredible snowshoes, exclaiming that he would "sail down his four-mile course at great speed, cross the ice frozen river, throw our mail toward the house, and glide out of sight, up and over a hill, by the momentum gathered in the three-mile descent."

The seemingly magical skiing postman captured the imaginations of children, who nearly hurt themselves trying to copy him with their makeshift sleds.

"The skis held to the track, but three of the kids went tumbling down a steep mountain," Wooster wrote, adding that when Thompson heard about the incident he returned to personally give the children a scolding.

During the harsh winter of 1867, an estimated 3,000 travelers were stranded all winter at Meadow

Lake City. They relied on Thompson to deliver their letters from home.

Snowshoe Thompson wasn't a wealthy man, but he enjoyed a rich life. He married Agnes Singleton of England in 1866, and a year later the couple's only child was born. They named him Arthur Thomas Thompson, and the family settled onto land that Thompson homesteaded in Diamond Valley less than thirty miles from the new state capital at Carson City, Nevada. As you might expect, Snowshoe Thompson's son learned to ski as soon as he could walk.

Thompson had become a respected member of his community whose name was well known throughout the region. He continued to work on

Thompson hand-carved a cradle for his son, Arthur.

the ranch, and he also served on the Alpine County (California) Board of Supervisors.

By 1868, the first railroad tracks were complete. After nearly twenty years on the trail, Thompson's regular services were no longer needed. Isolated mining camps and pioneer outposts remained in the hills, however, and he made special deliveries for pay from private contracts. But the bulk of his work was finished.

The time was long overdue for Thompson to be properly compensated by the government, and now he had his winter free to seek it.

Although the postmaster in Placerville, California, who was his supervisor, had never received official approval to hire him, Thompson had trusted that eventually the federal government would do the right thing. Members of the Nevada Legislature tried to help. During the 1869 session, state lawmakers signed a resolution and sent it to Washington, DC, calling on the US Congress to compensate Thompson the money he was owed.

As time passed, Thompson remained hopeful. Surely all officials in Washington, DC, needed was a little encouragement, he thought. He decided to travel to the nation's capital to see for himself. He carried with him a petition signed by 1,000 of his grateful friends, neighbors, and postal customers.

He set off in late January 1872 for the East, this time on the same train that had helped to put him out of a job. Even a man of Snowshoe's energy couldn't be expected to walk all the way to the nation's capital. Something happened on the way that only increased Thompson's legend.

Outside of Laramie, Wyoming, the train ran into an enormous snowstorm, which closed the tracks and caused a delay that promised to last several days. The snow, of course, did not intimidate Thompson. He decided to travel on foot for Laramie and was joined by another passenger. In a few hours, his confident companion tired and decided to turn back, but Snowshoe easily marched all the way, no doubt singing Norwegian folk songs.

Another problem greeted him at Laramie. The snow had delayed all travel in the area, and the next train heading east was fifty miles away in Cheyenne, Wyoming. True to his nature, Thompson smiled and kept on walking. He had an appointment to keep in Washington, DC, and wasn't about to be deterred by a few feet of snow or temperatures that dipped to near zero degrees.

Thompson reached Cheyenne in time to catch the train to Washington, DC. Upon arriving, he found the place strange and wonderful, but very frustrating. People were very busy, but his business moved very slowly. Finally, when the appointed time came Thompson met with committee members in an effort to receive his compensation. He called a witness from Placerville to testify on his behalf.

Thompson's home as it stood in the 1920s.

He wrote simple letters and sent a telegram to Agnes to update her on his progress. Like most fathers, he reminded his young son, Arthur, to listen his mother. He wrote in part, "Arthur, you must be a good boy and mind what Mother and Grand Mother tells you, then I will be so pleased when I come home and have them tell me about how good you have been."

He believed his meeting with the congressional committee went well. Members of Congress thanked him for his tireless work. He returned to Genoa and Diamond Valley and waited for news that never came.

Although the Nevada Legislature's resolution was approved by members of the House and considered by the Senate Committee on Post Offices and Post Roads in 1872, the Senate failed to act on. It has been speculated that the heavy toll of the Civil War and the nation's effort to rebuild the damaged country, known as Reconstruction, prevented the Senate to set aside the funds despite his loyal service.

Without a contract, he couldn't enforce his claim for payment. The figure he was owed was $6,000. He returned feeling beaten. The man who never seemed to tire felt fatigued by the disappointment. He would die without ever receiving payment from the federal government.

When Thompson arrived back home, his friends and neighbors collected money on his behalf. They knew the indispensible role he had played in their lives. In addition to delivering the mail for two decades, he often helped his neighbors plant their crops, graze their cattle and pasture their horses. Although he claimed he was not much of a farmer, he grew many crops and dug an irrigation ditch to bring water to the fields of Diamond Valley. Area ranchers still use the canal today.

Kindness was Snowshoe Thompson's greatest strength. Genoa postmaster S. A. Kinsey spoke for many when he said, "Most remarkable man I ever knew, that Snowshoe Thompson. He must be made of iron. Besides, he never thinks of himself, but he'd give his last breath for anyone else—even a total stranger."

In addition to tending his ranch, late in his life Thompson also managed the Pittsburg Mine in the high mountains above his home. When the miners

Thompson, sometimes spelled Thomson, is buried in Genoa, NV.

ran low on food, Thompson would carry a heavy pack full of provisions, including a quarter of beef, up the steep mountainside. Then he would ski back home.

John "Snowshoe" Thompson, legendary Sierra Mailman, died on May 15, 1876 after suffering from appendicitis. He was forty-nine years old. A pair of skis is etched on his gravestone with the epitaph, "Gone, but not forgotten."

Thompson's legend continued to grow after his death. When the Winter Olympics came to Squaw Valley, California, in the Eastern Sierra Nevada in 1960, Thompson's skiing innovation and personal courage were honored. For many years an annual Sierra Snowshoe Thompson Memorial Ski Race through valleys he named Faith, Hope, Charity, and

Diamond was popular with a new generation of cross-country skiers.

In 1975, Congressman Alphonzo Bell of California reflected on Thompson's importance and the injustice of the failure to compensate him in his lifetime. "By his act of bravery," Bell wrote, " 'Snowshoe' alone maintained communication with the outside world for the otherwise totally isolated residents of the Carson Valley and maintained vital mail service between East and West through the deep winter snow blanket over the Sierra Nevada."

Historians consider him a "founding father" of snow skiing in California. More than a century after his death, visitors to Placerville, Squaw Valley, and Genoa will find handsome statues dedicated to Snowshoe Thompson.

One bronze sculpture by Angus Kent Lamar stands ten feet high and graces the Boreal Ridge not far from where the real Snowshoe Thompson once delivered the mail throughout the winter. Dedicated on May 15, 1976, on the centennial of his death, it depicts the intrepid Sierra Nevada Mailman. One year earlier Congressman Bell submitted a bill to his colleagues to support the sculpture project. His request was for $6,000 from the US Treasury, the amount Thompson had been owed a century earlier.

Appendix:

In Praise of Snowshoe Thompson

From journalist and author Dan DeQuille: "He flew down the mountainside. . . . He did not ride astride his pole or drag it to one side as was the practice of other snowshoers, but held it horizontally before him after the manner of tightrope walker. His appearance was graceful, swaying his balance pole to one side and the other in the manner that a soaring eagle dips its wings."

From the *Sacramento Union* newspaper: "Mr. John A. Thompson left Carson Valley on Tuesday morning and reached this city at noon yesterday. He was three days and a half in coming through from Carson Valley and used on the snow the Norwegian skates, which are manufactured of wood."

From Evelyn Dangberg Teal, 1960: "Snowshoe's winter mail route became famed throughout the West. He was respected for his courage and venerated for saving many people from cold death in the mountains."

Glossary

Cape Horn: A far southern locale at the tip of Chile in South America.

Carcass: the body of a dead animal.

Northern Paiute: Native American tribe living in Northern Nevada largely displaced by emigrants.

Isthmus of Panama: A narrow section of land in Panama that links North and South America. It provided a short cut for travelers attempting to reach the Pacific Ocean but avoid traveling much further south and around Cape Horn.

Pack animals: Mules and horses used to pack a variety of goods and merchandise long distances, sometimes through the Sierra Nevada.

Sierra Nevada: Spanish for "Snow-covered mountain range."

Telegraph: Before the invention of the telephone, the telegraph system enabled persons to transmit messages over long distances by sending a series of simple coded signals over an electrified wire.

Cast of Characters

Elias "Lucky" Baldwin: Adventurer, investor, prospector, and horse breeder, he reported being rescued during a snowstorm by Thompson.

Christopher "Kit" Carson: Pathfinder, explorer of the West, guide for Capt. John C. Frémont.

Dan DeQuille: Noted frontier journalist based in Virginia City and an early chronicler of the efforts of Snowshoe Thompson, which helped make the letter carrier a legend.

Donner Party: An ill-fated group of emigrants led by brothers Jacob and George Donner, who traveled from Springfield, Illinois in the spring of 1846 bound for California. After making the mistake of attempting to travel over the Sierra in winter, the group became stranded. Of the 81 people in the party, only 45 survived.

John C. Frémont: American military officer and prolific explorer. His expedition produced maps that were considered essential to opening up the West. He was also a politician.

John Calhoun Johnson: Early mail carrier in the Sierra, replaced by Thompson. Johnson became a lawyer and judge in frontier Nevada and is probably best remembered as the namesake of the "Johnson Cutoff" through the Sierra.

Peter Skene Ogden: Born in Canada, he was a fur trader and is known as an early explorer in the West.

John Reese: A Salt Lake City businessman considered a founder of Mormon Station near the future site of Genoa, Nevada.

Agnes Singleton: She married Snowshoe Thompson in 1866.

James Sissons: A stranded packer who was rescued by Thompson. Sissons lost his legs to frostbite.

Clarence Wooster: Early telegraph operator and booster of Snowshoe Thompson.

Selected Bibliography and Further Reading

DeQuille, Dan. *The Big Bonanza: An Authentic Account of the Discovery, History and Working of the Comstock Lode*. Nevada Publications: Las Vegas, 1983.

DeQuille. *Washoe Rambles*. Westernlore Press: Los Angeles, 1963.

Dwyer, Richard A. and Richard E. Lingenfelter. *Dan DeQuille, the Washoe Giant: A Biography and Anthology*. University of Nevada Press: Reno, 1990.

Margo, Elizabeth. *Women of the Gold Rush*. Indian Head Books: New York, 1955.

Tortorich, Frank. *John A. "Snowshoe" Thompson: Pioneer Mail Carrier of the Sierra*. Pronghorn Press: Greybull, Wyoming, 2015.

Writers' Program, Work Projects Administration. *Nevada: A Guide to the Silver State*. Binfords & Mort: Portland, Ore., 1940.

Zanjani, Sally. *Devils Will Reign: How Nevada Began*. University of Nevada Press: Reno, 2007.

Websites

Author's Note: Undoubtedly one of the most informative websites is snowshoethompson.org, which is entirely dedicated to celebrating the legend and history of Thompson, helping to keep his amazing story alive for a new generation. My other favorite site that provides entertainment and insight is:

"Snowshoe Thompson: Legendary Skiing Mailman." Thestormking.com: https://thestormking.com/Sierra_Stories/Snowshoe_Thompson/snowshoe_thompson.html

Questions for Discussion

1. Imagine that you are sending a letter to a family member or a friend back in Snowshoe Thompson's day. What will you tell them about the mailman of the Sierra Nevada?

2. What impact did Thompson's skill on skis have on those who saw him?

3. What fear did Thompson have to overcome while on the trail?

4. Imagine that you are filling Thompson's pack. What would you put in it to help you through the Sierra winter?

5. What prepared Thompson for his job of delivering the mail in winter?

6. How has communication changed since Thompson's time?

7. What made the Sierra Nevada so difficult for travelers?

8. Using the facts contained in this story, what kind of adventure can you create?

9. If you had a chance to meet him today, what questions would you ask Snowshoe Thompson about his life?

10. Thompson did more than deliver the mail. What other jobs and duties did he have?

About the Author

Native Nevadan John L. Smith is a longtime journalist and the author of more than a dozen books. He has won many state, regional, and national awards for his writing and was inducted into the Nevada Press Association Newspaper Hall of Fame in 2016, the same year that saw him honored with the James Foley/Medill Medal for Courage in Journalism, the Society of Professional Journalists Ethics Award, and the Ancil Payne Award for Ethics in Journalism from the University of Oregon. He freelances for a variety of publications, including *The Nevada Independent.* The father of a grown daughter, Amelia, he is married to the writer Sally Denton and makes his home in Boulder City, Nevada.